Kicking Off

Fiona Park

chipmunkapublishing
the mental health publisher

Fiona Park

Published by
Chipmunkapublishing
United Kingdom

http://www.chipmunkapublishing.com

Copyright © 2015 Fiona Park

ISBN   978-1-78382-185-3

Author Biography

My name is Fiona Park. I am 59 years of age. I suffer from bi polar affective disorder. I had an idyllic childhood. My father played the violin and my mother sang as she performed her household chores. My head was always buried in a book. When I was fourteen my mother stopped singing. My father was diagnosed with paranoid schizophrenia and my mother had a nervous breakdown with the strain. My solution was to buy a ticket for London at the nearest railway station. As I embarked on the train, the railway police stopped me and marched me down the platform. I was one of the lucky ones.

In my twenties I was struck down with bi polar affective disorder. I was as mad as a hatter and I felt my life was shattered. After a disastrous marriage and an even more disastrous engagement I approached the big 4-0 by moving into a flat, procuring a job and living in the land of takeaways, alcopops and one night stands. I partied all night and worked all day. After ten years I became ill. The land where the roses never fade beckoned but I pulled through and my friends cancelled the wreaths. I was too ill to work. I joined a writers group, explaining that I did not have a degree in English but I wanted to write. They informed me that I had a degree in life!

Fiona Park

Chapter 1 – The Family And Their Home

Welcome to the mad house, better known as the asylum. This consists of a rather grand Victorian house which is my home. Adjacent to this are many buildings magnificent in their grandeur. My ward is situated on the ground floor of the asylum, it is draughty. The ceilings are very high and the windows long in length, framing the picturesque view of the gardens. The massive grounds are well maintained and surrounded by country side. There are cherry and apple trees which are a picture of loveliness which warm the cockles of my heart when blossoming in spring. Throughout the seasons the patients are given the opportunity of walking in the grounds escorted by nursing staff. The fresh air is vibrant and rejuvenating, clearing the cobwebs. During the summer months this is a popular past time, however during the winter time a mug of tea and a woolly jumper seems a better alternative.

The year is 1978. My name is Iain and I suffer from paranoid schizophrenia. Committed as I am for life it is a case of 'till death do us part' but I would rather have a woman any day.

During the Suez Crisis I fought for my country having a piece of shrapnel lodged in my neck; however I don't feel much like a war hero now. I twitch and shake with the long term use of drugs; they either dope me up with pills or pull my trousers down and inject my rear. I have what is known as tardive dyskinesia, 'side effect city', right enough.

Hearing voices as I do can be very frightening. This is an illness of the mind, very real to me. I see snakes climbing up my legs and I live in fear. I wonder where the fun is in life.

Then there is Rose, who sits opposite me in the day room. She has peach skin, curly brown hair and piercing blue eyes, now that I could go for in a big way. Rose lived in the islands off the coast of Scotland. Her family were very strict and religious. When my peach got pregnant before she was married, they shipped her down to the asylum in shame. Rose is not mad but the medication they give her causes twitching side effects, giving her the appearance of having a mental illness. My peach sits crying all day and saying that she wants to go home. Rose speaks Gaelic most of the time, shouting out for her mother in time of stress.

My shoes upset me, they are worn and laced up with string and I have holes in my socks. The friends I have had all my life, my family, they all dumped me. I am the 'loony' no body wants to know. I have feelings, I cry, I smile, I suffer, the pain I feel hurts. It is similar to the hurt when you see action, wondering if you will see your loved ones once more. However, I have no loved ones. This is Alpha, this is omega!

I have a dream that keeps me from going into the Bathroom and taking my leather belt off and swinging the night away. I dream Rose and I got married and went to Blackpool on honeymoon. I would need some new shoes, a smart suit and a bunch of flowers to propose. It is a fantasy, but when life is worthless, a dream in the bleakness of reality can give life meaning.

Every time the nurses walk in the room I grin, we all grin. Sometimes I can't do it, I feel too ill with the voices and I feel unwell, but I try so hard, we all do. If we all behave appropriately we get a token, this can be exchanged for a fag. It is called 'token economy therapy', but we don't care what it is called, as long as we get a fag. There are treats for non smokers such as sweets, drinks or a trip out. However most of us smoke. The patients who are well enough wash up the pots and pans with the nurses or do chores. They get a couple of tokens. The nurses sit smoking at the nurse's station as they complete their paperwork and give handovers on the running of the ward and any changes.

As I sit here a nurse walks in the room. I am struggling to grin and behave appropriately. I feel the raw emotions swell up inside me, and then the voices start. My face feels hot and a feel anger and fury at my constraint. I blow, kicking over the coffee table in the process. I stand up swearing. Two beefy nurses drag me away to the bedroom. Reinforcements arrive. I kicked off for freedom! Dragged on the bed, my trousers were pulled down and my rear injected. They held me down for a few minutes then their grip loosened.

I would not get a fag now, oh well bribery and corruption. When I was led back into the day room, everybody was sitting around the little black and white television, everything was back in place. I felt ashamed. To tell you the truth I do not see the point of switching the television on because no one ever hears it.

Nellie who has a behavioural problem screams out at various times during the day. Nellie is obviously in distress but it drives us even nuttier than we are. The room would be deadly quiet then the screaming would start. We would jump with the shock and the nurses would try to pacify her, to no avail. We had to remember she was ill, hard though this is.

Nellie had lived with her mother, father, brothers and sisters, however when Nellie became a certain age the government stopped her money. The family were poor and times were hard, hence Nellie was sent to the asylum.

I looked out the window, the taxi cars were there. The posh patients were going for afternoon tea. It was a trip once a week. I bet they have shiny polished shoes, not laced with string, shoes as shiny as I had worn in the services. A tear rolled down my cheek. Upset as I was about not getting a fag I wondered about the leather belt. No! I was in the services! They won't break me! Keep right on till the end of the road!

I was awakened from my melancholy state by a sight that left me with the blood rushing to my head. Willie was asking Miss Rose if she would like a biscuit. It was not what he said but the tone of his voice, the sleaze ball smile. 'Pistols at dawn!' was my immediate thought. I calmed myself down; it was a biscuit, not a wedding ring.

Now there is Willie, he self harmed himself. Talking about a pressure in his body; caused by worry, stress and anxiety. He said it was so great and over powering. The only relief was to cut himself. Willie's scars were mostly hidden by his clothes fortunately. He had been drinking heavily, neglecting himself. His personal hygiene had suffered. He was not washing himself, eating properly or cleaning his home. Willies neighbours called the doctors in. He was committed for life. Willie had worked as an electrician down the mines. He worked all night at this job then during the day he worked at a private job rewiring a bowling alley. Willie wanted the best for his family; however the pressure of no sleep and deep concentration at work overwhelmed him. His body bursting with pressure he turned to self harm. Willie's wife left him and he lost his family. Talking of his mother and her unconditional love, he said his mother would visit every day if she was alive. I was willing to adopt Willie into the family, the family where mental illness is the norm.

I looked over and saw Maggie sitting in the corner, the nurse's pet who suffered from dementia. Maggie had started smoking fags at the age of fourteen. She had smoked all her life. Maggie asked the nurses for a smoke and they took one of her tokens and exchanged it for a fag. The nurses lit it for her, however she took one puff saying her chest was burning and she tasted acid in her mouth, complaining her hiatus hernia was the problem. However five minutes later she was asking once more for a smoke. Her poor short term memory caused this. Maggie was singing the song "What a Wonderful World" sung by Louis Armstrong. I wondered for a moment if she knew something that I did not. Maggie's hands were moving rhythmically in time to the words and the performance was to say the least, uplifting. Maggie was a very sweet old lady and we all loved her. After talking to Maggie a few times, I realised that she had a brilliant memory of the past; however she had no recollection of what happened a few hours ago or a few weeks ago. The dear sweet little lady had a good long term memory but a poor short term memory. It was wonderful to hear her stories of how she had worked in the fields. Potato picking was her favourite story and parsnip picking when she lived in England. The nurses adored Maggie but they tilted her chair back and put her feet on the stool because she kept trying to escape. The potato picking must have started and the fresh crisp air must have beckoned, not the constant smell of bleach from the cleaning of the ward. We all would like to escape but the ward was a locked ward and all the nurses had keys. We were outcasts of society and had nowhere to go.

Living alone as she did there were problems of Maggie leaving the gas cooker on and leaving the front door open and walking about in the middle of the night. Her husband was deceased, there was no one, hence she was committed.

The group would not be complete without Rab 'the paper fag king'. He makes cigarettes out of paper and smokes them. I suppose needs must. All over the ward there are pieces of burnt paper. Lots of people in the hospital smoke paper fags but I like tobacco in mine, so I will try and smile and grin and get a token from the nurses that I can exchange for a fag. Rab suffers from manic depression and is psychotic most of the time. He has periods where he is elated and other times he sits with his head in his hands suffering from deep depression, mental illness is a family trait. Rab told me his father had a serious mental illness. Rab never married or had family. He was taken ill before his life really blossomed into any pattern away from psychiatrists or mental health. Rab's mother was looking after her husband, therefore when Rab got ill he was committed. The powers that be, said the strain would be too much for her nursing two mentally ill people.

This concludes my family who I will live with, breathe with, laugh with and eventually die with. In the darkness of the night as I lie incarcerated in my institution bed; I ask god why he has punished me in such a cruel manner. I pray for a miracle. Not for riches or cars, I pray for my freedom. I fought on foreign shores for freedom but I lost my own, god help me.

Chapter 2 – The Psychiatrist That Knows His Stuff

Today is the ward round on our ward. We will meet with our psychiatrist and discuss our state of mind, problems, medication and how we feel about life in general.

My psychiatrist is called Dr Gérard. When he walks down the corridor he has a presence. Wearing a pin striped suit, white shirt and tie and a gold pocket watch visible and gleaming. He looks every bit the part of the professional he is, and he is every bit as good as he looks. I would say that he is in his forties, receding hair and is of average build. Dr Gérard is unassuming; he seems unaware of his own brilliance. A good psychiatrist must be street wise, this must come through experience and I sensed he is not shocked easily. Over the years he has heard it all.

I talked about my past to him, my childhood, my career, my family and last of all my illness. Dr Gérard knew me. It was a famous saying in the hospital that Dr Gérard knew his patients. I have never heard a truer word. This one knew his stuff.

There was a hustle and bustle on the ward. The nurses were all rushing round and looked very efficient. The smell of bleach was worse than usual. We were all sitting around apprehensively waiting on Dr Gérard calling our name and the nurses escorting us for our consultation. As Maggie burst into song I felt as if I wanted to ask her what was so wonderful about our world. I refrained, 'each to their own'. How I longed for a coal fire with its glowing embers and comforting warmth as the flames flickered and danced soothing my troubled soul. Smoking my fag and drinking a mug of tea alone with my thoughts. I needed space, time to think, away from the constant noise. I compared the ward with Butlins and the nurses as red coats.

The nurse came in gave us all a token which we could exchange for a fag, our behaviour must have been good. As I waited patiently to see Dr Gérard, I smoked and I felt at peace. The nurses smoked at the nurse's station where they did their paperwork. They smoked in their dinner break, nearly all of them smoked. Must have been part of the job description. The nurse approached me and informed me that Dr Gérard was waiting to see me. There was a sense of expectation as I made my way down the long bleak corridor; my shoes clicking on the mosaic stone tiled floor. I knew Dr Gérard would emphasize with me, feel my agony, suffering in sheer hopelessness. Empathy and respect were second nature to him. As I entered the room Dr Gérard welcomed me. We chatted for a few minutes I felt comfortable telling Dr Gérard about my voices; telling me people were trying to steal my blood. This frightened me. He said he would increase the dosage of my injection and give me medication which should help. He said think about happy times in your life. We talked about my childhood. My father had come to Scotland during the potato famine in Ireland. My mother had eleven brothers and sisters. We were poor but always had food. At Christmas time, the presents were an apple and an orange. My mother made a suet dumpling and dried it off in front of the coal fire. We were happy. I had two sisters, however we lost touch, but I love them. We talked for a while about the ward. He asked me if I was settled. I proceeded to tell him I thought I was going to die. Sitting with my head down and an expression of sheer conviction; I awaited his response; "Not that one again!" Dr Gérard answered. I looked at him, we both burst out laughing. "I will see you soon, look after yourself" he said. I left the room smiling. There was a bounce in my step as I marched back to the day room and my arm chair. The family were very territorial; everyone has their own special chair, low and behold anyone who sat in someone else's chair.

Chapter 3 – Life Is Not A Bunch Of Roses!

As I sat at the red Formica table with my family, I proceeded to tuck into my bowl of lumpy porridge and drink my mug of stewed tea. We all queue up for breakfast, we queue up for dinner and we queue up for our tea. Becoming institutionalised we even queue up for ECT. Routine rules the roost. The asylum feels like home to the point where we could not cope in normal life. My family chatted as they ate their breakfast. Rab the paper fag king informed of his new found status; he was the Prime Minister, and was a very powerful figure. Rab told us he was soon to be a very rich person. He was going to buy us a castle to live in and we would have servants. I told Rab this was a delusion that we were happy to hear. I asked if there were free fags in our castle. I informed Rab; he could be Prime Minister any day, but he must stop saying the television is bugged and switching it off. We liked to watch crossroads and Coronation Street. I said the television was only a little black box and it was difficult at the best of times to watch a programme, with Willie pacing the floor and ringing his hands in a very agitated manner and Nellie constantly screaming. Rose blurted out that she would like to watch 'Top of the Pops'.

Rose had a hard time, she became angry and depressed; this was treated as an illness with drugs; however the anger and depression was not an illness. This was how she was feeling in herself; her mood, her struggle to cope with her commitments. This was how Rose normally felt.

Maggie was munching on her toast, she told the nurses there was no sugar in her tea, and then informed them that she liked six tea spoons full. They gave her more and more, not wanting to upset their pet. Maggie was constantly putting her coat and hat on, saying that she had to go and catch her bus home. Then she would go to the ward door and rattle the handle, screaming, saying that she wanted to go home. The nurses hid her coat and hat. Maggie felt the cold. She was always shouting at the nurses to put more coal on the fire. An impossible scenario as the building was heated by under floor heating.

Sinking into my day dream world, I visualised myself in the snug bar of 'the Rovers Return' with a glass of stout. Suddenly my fantasy crushed into desolation, it was as if a bomb had dropped. There was a crashing sound. I looked towards Willie; he had smashed his tea cup. He proceeded to slash his arms and wrists with the sharp piece of crockery that he had acquired. His features were tight and his eyes were deeply intense, reflecting his desperation; shouting 'relief!' as he attacked his arms in a heated rage. The nurses raised the alarm, two heavy weight male orderlies ran in. 'Stupid bastard' I shouted. Rose's hands were covering her face. Maggie and Nellie were screaming. Rab was crying. The male orderlies grabbed the chair from behind to avoid confrontation. They pulled Willie and the chair to the other end of the room. They then grabbed Willie's shoulders from behind and shouted 'Drop it'. Willie dropped the piece of crockery. They draped towels over his arms and marched him to the treatment room. The nurses escorted us to our arm chairs. The experience left us all shaken. The staff made us cups of sweet tea, and tried their best to re-assure us, they supported and consoled us. A nurse with a mops and bucket appeared and cleared away the evidence of Willies self harm episode.

Sitting in my armchair, I cast my eyes over the view from the windows. The grass glistened with winter frost and the trees glittered in the morning light. Roof tops sparkling as the snow flakes fell. Everything was pure white. The foot prints in the snow, now sleet, spoiled the illusion. Winter had arrived. Soon the crisp and crunchy shimmering surfaces will bring with it freezing temperatures. I will look out the window, a barrier to the icy weather.

A nurse awoke me from my thoughts, she said there were some clothes in my room that might fit me, would I like to come and try them on for size. Someone must have died, was my immediate reaction. I hoped it was someone from the posh ward. If someone dies and their clothes are in good condition, they are passed on to someone of the same size and build. I followed the nurse down the corridor, she unlocked my bedroom door. I followed her into the room. Laid on the bed were some clothes, nice checked shirts, trousers (not worn), socks without holes, what appeared to be a Harris Tweed overcoat and new braces, still in the packet. The nurse informed me that she would stand at the door and I was to let her know if I needed any help. Everything fitted. I could be smart again, like a soldier on parade; pity about my shabby shoes. The clothes were sent to the laundry to be labelled with my name. I thanked her; she was not a bad sort. Shuffling behind her, we returned to the day room and my arm chair. Later that day the nurses informed us that Willie was none the worse for wear for his experience. We were relieved but the trauma that we had suffered was not forgotten. However we all retired to bed emotional but reassured.

As we sat at breakfast the next day, Willie crept stealthily into the room. He had a sheepish look on his face, his head hung low as if in disgrace. I sensed that he was unsure of his welcome into the fold. He wore a long sleeved shirt, however thick crepe bandages peered beneath the cuff. Willie sat in his arm chair awaiting any response, positive or otherwise. 'I had to get relief' Willie shouted. 'Enough, forget it Willie, we all have problems that is why we are in the asylum. We are all ill people'.

Fiona Park

Chapter 4 – Preparation for Christmas

The month of December has arrived, triggering thoughts of the forth coming Christmas. My expectation is low, as I reflect on my memories of last Christmas. I do not want to hope for too much, in case I am hurt and suffer disappointment. I will attempt to paint a short picture of my experience of last Christmas. This was spent in a long stay ward, where the patients had no one to advocate for them. I feel grief and sadness saying that the staff's behaviour reflected the fact that they were in it for the money. Not the rewards of caring for people. I was moved to the present ward last new year. Christmas day was the same as many Saturdays or Sundays, with no planned activities and routine being the theme. Not one member of staff wished me a Happy Christmas, we were ignored as the staff laughed and chatted amongst themselves. As I sat in my chair looking out the window, I saw well patients' kissing and cuddling their families, as they were taken home for the day. I tried to feel happy for them, but I had a sinking feeling in my gut and I was overcome by my own hopelessness; the hopelessness of my situation. There was a Christmas tree sparsely decorated but the nurses had not watered it and the needles were all over the carpet. As we stood in the queue for Christmas dinner I remembered the lovely food they served, it tasted as good as it looked. The kitchen staff had taken a pride in their work, a lot better than normal. As I sat in my chair I remembered the expresses on the faces of the patients, expressions of sheer gloom and misery. I wondered why the nurses did not put some music on; we had a record player and records. I decided that it was maybe too much trouble for them. Reiterating my previous statement; that they were in the job for the money. Christmas day passed, just another day to get through.

As I sat in my arm chair, the strangest thing happened; one of the nurses came in the room with little tubs and brushes and started painting Christmas pictures on the windows. Well I never, I thought. We were all enthralled, at first I thought I was imagining things but no, this was real. Good for her I thought. I felt warm inside, thinking that this might be the start of something; the build up to a Good Christmas. However I decided that it may be a one off situation. I did not want to raise my hopes, as the day progressed there was a Santa, then a Christmas tree, then Christmas bells and a Christmas stocking painted on the windows. Nobody really cared about television. We were happy to watch the transformation of our windows. Maybe these nurses would water the Christmas tree. I wished I could buy the family presents. I decided that I would take everybody out in a taxi and buy them afternoon tea. Now Rose. I would buy her something special, a jewellery box with a revolving ballerina and it would play music; of course there would be some pretty jewellery in it. I fell asleep.

As I walked into the day room the next morning, Rab told me to look at what was happening, Rose pointed to the walls and Maggie of course thought it was a wonderful world. Willie shouted 'paper chains'. I looked at the walls. The nurses were decorating them with paper chains. Chains made with loops of coloured paper. The nurses informed me that the patients in the asylum had made the paper chains. They were draped and hung everywhere; the room portrayed the magic of Christmas. The nurses said 'maybe after breakfast you could go to the Occupational Therapy room and help make a Christmas cake. Rose was obviously pleased; she said that she would like to go. Rab said he would go. Willie said that baking cakes was woman's work; he said that he had never baked a cake in his life and he was not starting now. Nellie was not well enough; screaming out as usual. Maggie said that she had to go for her bus. 'Christmas cake indeed'! Willie shouted. I thought I would tag along with Rose and Rab (more Rose than Rab). Baking cakes was something I had never done either; oh well, first time for everything. I am good at licking the bowl.

Later on that morning, the Occupational Therapist came into the day room to collect her helpers. 'Who's coming to bake the Christmas cake?' she said. Rose put her hand in the air and proceeded to make her way up the corridor, then Rab. I clip clopped behind them. Suddenly Rab, who was walking in front of me, turned round and accused me of following him. He was waving his arms in the air and shouting in a very aggressive manner, he was going to make mince meat of me. The nurse sounded the alarm, nurses from other wards arrived; we made our way back down the corridor. Rab was screaming and swearing. A member of staff restrained him, hustled him into his room, where a nurse sat outside his door on a chair. I had a lucky escape I thought, he would cool down. It is the asylum we live in after all, he is ill, but I must admit I am shaken. As I sat down in my arm chair the nurses approached me. They seemed concerned; they made me a cup of tea. Rose shouted to me 'are you alright Ian?' 'Yes Rose' I answered, we will not be baking any cake today. Rose looked visibly upset; the nurses were fussing over her. Rab the 'Paper fag King' right enough! As I sat in my armchair, I mulled over memories of happy times, as my mother and two sisters and I walked over the snow clad fields during the winter time, ever Sunday we walked. There was no money for expensive past times. Walking was free and good for the soul.

The next day after breakfast I was sitting drinking my stewed tea when the door swung open and a male orderly from another ward made a grand entrance, he was a big muscly chap and was carrying a Christmas tree. Behind him a nurse carried a bucket with earth in it. 'Soon sort this out' he proclaimed. I was transfixed on the scene before me. First the orderly lifted the tree and secured it in the bucket. It kept wobbling too and fro, his solution was to collect stones from the garden which fixed the tree in place. One of the nurses covered the bucket in Christmas paper with the aid of scissors and sellotape. A few strands of tinsel were used to decorate the tree. It was the icing on the cake. That is a sore point, best forget about cakes. The room reminded me of Santa's grotto, with the paper chains, painted windows and the Christmas tree, these nurses were a bunch of good ones.

The snow was lying on the grounds, snow flakes were falling as a nurse played an LP of Christmas music, and I felt warm and content. My troubles were melting, as snow melts in a thaw. For a short period of time I was free from voices and snakes. However, as Christmas comes around every year, sure as fate, I will not be unburdened for a long stretch of time. Make hay while the snow falls. Today was Christmas Eve. As I looked across at Rose, this Christmas Eve, I thought the only thing missing from the grotto was mistletoe. I could hold it above her head and give her a big smacker on the cheek. Maybe dreams are for losers. As the doors swung open into the day room, lightening struck! Two nurses are pushing a trolley with bottles of alcohol stacked on it, 'Anyone like a drink' they shouted merrily. 'What you got?' Willie shouted. 'Whisky, vodka, martini, cans of beer', they replied. Willie had a beer. Rose sipped a martini. They worked their way around then I asked for whiskey. The nurses gave the smokers fags, and then they poured themselves a drink and sat down beside us and lit a cigarette. The nurses raised their glassed and said 'Cheers,'. We chatted amongst ourselves, the nurses said that they were off on Christmas day, and were going home to wrap presents; they said they had vegetables to peel and trifle to make. We all had another drink. Rose started singing a song from the islands, she had a beautiful voice. Rab said he could not stay for Christmas, he had a country to run, him being Prime Minister of course. Maggie started singing 'what a wonderful world'. We all joined in singing. We all knew the words, as we had heard them so many times. The nurses were singing too. After two whiskeys, Nellie's screams seem melodic. Good measures I will tell you. Willie looked content; the beers must have gone down a treat. Later on I was escorted to my room and snuggled into my covers like a 'bug in a rug'. My mothers saying, 'god bless' her.

Chapter 5 – Christmas Day

As I woke early on Christmas morning, the room was in complete darkness; however the light from the glass panel above my bedroom door filtered rays of light into my room. A package on my bed was revealed. Curious as I was to discover its contents, I switched the light on, the package was wrapped in Christmas paper and for the life of me I did not know why a present was on my bed. I presumed at first that there had been a mistake, but after close observation my name was printed on the label. Half asleep I unravelled the wrapping paper, and then a very mysterious cardboard box appeared. As I lifted the lid of the box a bomb exploded. There before me was a pair of black shiny shoes, tied up with laces, not string. I lifted one out; the soles of the shoes had not been worn. I looked at the label on the box, they were my size. Slipping them on my feet they fitted perfectly. I had felt so bad for such a long time wearing my worn shoes. I felt as if I was not only a pauper but also that I lived in shame. I had been a proud man all my days and now with my new shoes I would have a little of my dignity back. I hurt inside at what this mental illness had made me suffer; thank you god for my shoes. Feeling a bit emotional I decided to get dressed for breakfast and see the family, but first I had a little ceremony to perform. Walking over to my chest of drawers, I opened the top drawer. Slipping my hand in right to the back I pulled out a piece of sack cloth. Unwrapping it, a deep blue regal, and velvet bag appeared. When the tie was undone I slipped my fingers inside, pulling out two military medals. Today is Christmas day and I will pin the medals on my shirt and wear them with pride. As my commanding officer pinned them on my uniform, I had served my country and felt proud of my achievements, especially in the Suez Crisis.

The Suez Crisis was an invasion of Egypt in late 1956, by Israel, followed by Britain and France. The aims were to gain western control of the Suez Canal and remove President Nassar from power. Pressure from the United States, Russia and the United Nations forced a cease fire. President Nassar's status in the Arab world was very high after British troops left Egypt; ending 74 years of occupation. This contributed to the resignation of Prime Minister Anthony Eden.

A quick inspection before I marched out of my bedroom, down the corridor and into the day room and the family. I checked that my medals were pinned on securely and made my way to my arm chair. I smiled; I was a sight for sore eyes. Thanks to my medals, new shoes and the bereavement in the posh ward. I don't have any holes in my socks, thanks to them. May they rest in peace. I walked into the day room and sat in my arm chair. The family were all present and correct. The nurses commented on my appearance and were fascinated by my medals. They joked about Santa bringing me new shoes. Christmas carols were playing on the record player and I wished everyone a Happy Christmas.

As we ate our breakfast I asked everyone what they had received for a present. Rose said that she was given perfume, soap, bubble bath and talc. Willie and Rab got socks. Nellie and Maggie did not reply. Nellie was too busy screaming and Maggie was busy persuading the nurses to give her 6 sugars in her tea. As the family left the breakfast table and walked back to their chairs I was aware of a clanking noise. I looked behind me and there was a knife on the floor. 'It's fallen out of Willie's pocket!' Rose shouted. The nurses raised the alarm and before Willie could bend and pick it up it was swept up quick as a flash by staff. Willie was marched to his room screaming and a nurse sat outside his door. He must have sneakily acquired it from the breakfast trolley. 'Merry Christmas to you too Willie!' I thought, sarcastically.

Today was the Christmas day that the nurses had worked towards; decorated windows, paper chains, Christmas tree and all the shopping for presents. Good on them. I even caught a nurse watering the Christmas tree. Today was Christmas day, it was a white Christmas. As we all sat watching the little black and white television, I felt a sense of belonging as I glanced at the family. Rab 'the paper fag king' started shouting at me and accused me of staring at him. Informing him that this was a lot of rubbish and we did not want this on Christmas day. He asked me if I knew who he was and told me that I should not talk to him n this way. I said; 'you are Prime Minister Rab' 'Exactly, show respect!' Rab replied. I shook my head, the situation was defused. We all had a smoke.

As we sat down to eat our Christmas dinner Willie appeared. He sat at the table and was very quiet. The meal was really nice; turkey with all the trimmings followed by Christmas pudding and custard. We all chatted as we ate our meal. 'My compliments to the chef' I joked. After our meal we retired to our arm chairs. Very soon after the strangest thing happened; a nurse entered the room carrying a wooden chair. Walking behind her was a woman of small build. She looked thin and frail. She wore a woolly hat, a thick coat with a scarf wrapped around her neck and furry boots. The nurse shouted that Rab had a visitor. Walking up to Rab with the chair she plonked it next to him. He looked at the woman, she looked at him, then sheer un cut emotion took over. He stood up, arms out stretched, his bottom lip quivering and shouted out 'Mother'. 'Robert' she replied. They gript and help each other as if there was no tomorrow, tears running down their cheeks.

I felt so happy for Rab; his mother visiting him on Christmas day. The scene before me made me feel emotional. To tell you the truth we were all gobsmacked. Rab's mum took her coat off and sat down on the wooden chair. They held each others hands. Rab's mum talked of her love for Rab and the worry she had felt knowing he was in the asylum. Rab's mum told Rab that his dad had died. A few more tears were shed. Rab asked if he could go home with her and leave the asylum. She explained that she did not keep well and was not well enough to look after him. He was upset but accepted this. They cuddled again and wiped each others tears. Rab's mum told him that she had bought him a present; a Christmas cake she had baked for him. She reached in her bag and brought out a cake wrapped in foil. 'Share it with the other patients tonight with your cups of tea' she said. A nurse came and took the Christmas cake, promising her that everyone would have a piece tonight. I thought to myself 'We're having a Christmas cake are we? And we don't have to bake it. You are forgiven Rab!'. Rab's mum stayed quite a while. She then told Rab she had to get home before darkness set in. 'I will come again my beloved son' she said. She proceeded to put her coat and hat on and her scarf. She asked the nurses if they would open the door. She kissed Rab goodbye and the nurses escorted her as she left. Rab started shouting 'Don't go mother!' but she was gone. Rab sat with his head in his hands crying.

That Christmas evening, as freezing temperatures hit the area and snow blizzards took their toll, the asylum did not seem such a miserable place to be. The arrival of the drinks trolley with its alcohol and Christmas cake confirmed this. The nurses poured us all a drink, then they poured themselves one and we all had a fag. They said they were worried about getting home in the bad weather. After they had their drink they put some Christmas Carols on the record player, then they cut the Christmas cake. Placing it on small plates, they passed it to each of us. Rab told the nurses to have a piece of cake. It was delicious. I thanked Rab. Maggie was shouting for another sherry. Rab and Willie had a couple of stiff drinks, ease the trauma a little. I looked across at Rose; she had a piece of tinsel wrapped round her head. She was sipping a martini. I asked her if she'd enjoyed her Christmas. 'I live here' she said. 'And Christmas was nice; however it is not my home. I am shamed; I will never see the island or my family again'. I told Rose there was nothing I could say to take away the pain. She nodded her head in agreement. Nellie was screaming, it was her Christmas too. I must try not to be irritated. I asked Maggie if she had always taken six sugars in her tea. 'During the war'; Maggie informed me, 'sugar was rationed, I never had any sugar to put in my tea. When the war ended I was so pleased to have sugar that I started putting teaspoons full in my tea.' Good for you Maggie, I thought.

As I drank my whiskey I looked at my shoes, then at Rose, then at the decorated room and the family. I did not want to forget today. I wanted a clear picture in my head to look back on. I decided it was late; the nurses escorted me to my bedroom. I unpinned my medals, wrapped them up and put them safe in my drawer. I undressed and went to bed. I fell asleep.

Chapter 6 – New Year

Tonight is New Years Eve, there is a sense of expectance as we sip our drinks, smoke our fags and await midnight and the timing of Big Ben on our television. As I look out the window at the grand Victorian buildings, I wonder if the nobility had lived here many years ago; or maybe Rab lived here in a past life when he was Prime Minister. Boundless and uninviting snow falls, I long for the smell of freshly cut grass and lavender scent. Apple trees laden with blossom in the spring time, chirping birds and the warm night air, long summer days. The Scottish music playing on the record player lifted my spirits. A nurse came round with short bread and we all had another drink. I looked around me, soon the Christmas tree, the paper chains and the painted windows would all be a thing of the past.

Happiness, translucent yet intangible had fallen on me. Not cold and bitter as snow but warm and up lifting; an answer to a prayer. I looked at Rose, then Willie then Rab, Nellie and Maggie. The family were happy and correct. Then suddenly the fire alarm sounded, all hell broke loose. Nurses shouting 'Fire!, We have to evacuate the building'. The family just sat sipping their drinks and smoking, saying that it was a lot of rubbish! Then nurses appeared wheeling piles of trollies overflowing with blankets. The Fire Brigade have been called. They are on their way. Suddenly two male orderlies appeared and told us that we had to make our way to the fire exit door at the rear end of the day room. They helped everyone out of their chairs and we were covered in blankets and they told us to leave the building. We all complained 'It's snowing! It's cold!' He replied 'the asylums on fire, you don't have any choice!'

We all made our way outside, moaning and asking what was going on. We were in shock. There was lots of staff with us in case anyone decided to make a quick get away. I had blankets around my head and my shoulders, however my face was cold. Maggie needed someone holding her arm, she was ready to escape.

'Is the asylum really on Fire?' Willie said. Rab ran up to the window of the building, knocked on it and said, 'Let me in, I am Prime Minister!' staff brought him back shouting. Rose looked like an Eskimo princess wrapped in her blankets. Nellie's screams were even worse than usual. Then suddenly the door swung open in the posh ward, all the patients were being evacuated one after one, covered in blankets. Escorted by staff, they made their way to the concrete driveway covered in snow.

Willie tried to make a quick dash for freedom, however the male orderly caught him and he was returned to the fold. I jumped up and down to keep warm and rubbed my hands together. I asked the male orderly standing next to me, what was the cause of the fire. He paused for a moment then he told me a nurse who was on her evening break was making herself some toast. She placed it in the toaster, switched it on, however she was called away to an emergency and forgot to switch it off. The toast went on fire, and then the toaster went on fire. The fire alarm sounded and the fire brigade were called. The building was evacuated. Just as he finished speaking, a fire engine with flashing lights made its way to the entrance of the building with its sirens bellowing. There was a magnificent cheer as the firemen climbed down from the wagon; carrying extinguishers and hoses they entered the building. 'Save our asylum!' Rab shouted, tears running down his cheeks. My face felt numb, the air was so cold it caught the back of my throat. I hoped the firemen would put the fire out before we all caught hypothermia.

Suddenly there was an almighty scream; 'Happy New Year' the nurses shouted 'It's the bells; Happy new year!' Everyone from the posh ward came rushing over shaking our hands and wishing us a Happy New Year. I rushed over to the family; I shook their hands wishing them a Happy New Years. The nurses were cuddling everyone and wishing them a Happy New Year. I shook their hands. One of the nurses piped up with 'Auld Lang Syne'. We held hands on this troubled night, the asylum bonded as we sang;

"Should auld acquaintance be forgot,
And never brought to mind?
Should auld acquaintance be forgot,
And Auld Lang Syne."

We cheered and pelted each other with snowballs, the moments passed slowly, until the main door to the asylum building swung open and the firemen appeared. 'The fire is out!' one of the firemen shouted. Everyone clapped their hands and cheered the brave men. They made their way towards us, shaking hands and wishing everyone a Happy New Year. The gratitude was evident as everyone thanked them and patted them on the back. They proceeded to tidy up their equipment then with a final wave they climbed into their cabin and drove away.

We were escorted up the stairs of the main entrance, bedraggled and cold we plodded our way down the stone mosaic corridor to the door of our ward. Escorted by nurses we made our way to the day room. Linen skips were brought in and the blankets that were no longer needed as a barrier from the cold winters evening were tossed to the wind. They had served their purpose, thank god they were no longer needed and our asylum had been saved.

The family sat down in their arm chairs, the nurses said they would bring us hot tea to warm us up but they would have to make it in a kitchen from another ward as our ward kitchen was out of bounds for a while. I thought to myself, the tea will be even more stewed than usual, or cold. I decided to be grateful for small mercies and not moan. The family were safe and the asylum was safe. Our home was beginning to warm up; it was a slow process as the firemen must have shut the power off. I longed for my hot cup of tea. The family looked exhausted; Maggie was not singing, Nellie was not screaming. The emotional trauma would hit them when they woke up later on today. If we ever get to bed that is. The nurses arrived with hot tea. It *was* hot, and not stewed. Wonders will never cease. The family drank their tea. They crawled to their bedrooms escorted by staff. This would be a new year never to be forgotten.

Fiona Park

Chapter 7 – No Peace in the Madhouse

The year is 1979, the month is January. Sitting in my arm chair after breakfast drinking my stewed tea, I am coughing and spluttering. My throat is sore and I have a headache. Looking across at Willie he is wheezing and barking. The nurses come over; they check our temperatures, informing us that we have flu. They say that there is a flu epidemic in the area and pack us off to bed.

I slept most of the day. The nurses brought medicines and drinks. My body ached and I felt tired. I fell asleep for the night but it was short lived. The agenda for this evening was commotion in the mad house. Nurses were shouting 'Willie is self harming'. The alarm sounded, the door to the ward swung open, reinforcements arrived. I heard the nurses say 'Willie has unscrewed a loose screw from his bed and was self harming himself with it!'

No peace even when you have flu in the madhouse I thought. The male orderly was asking Willie to hand the screw over. Eventually after much persuasion he complied. The nurse popped her head in the door and apologised for any disturbance. I thought all hell breaking loose is more than a disturbance. I asked if Willie was alright, 'Don't worry' the nurse said 'He will be fine; we will get him settled for the night'. Then she left. I fell asleep.

The next morning the nurse came with drinks and medicines. She informed me that Maggie and Rab had flu, and a few of the nurses. The nurse said that everyone was dropping like flies. She told me that she was working a double shift today as there was a staff shortage. I thought I might catch forty winks but I could here Maggie banging on the ward door shouting that she had to get home to her mother. A nurse escorted her to her room and sat with her. I was worried about Maggie, she is old and frail. She is a fighter but flu can be serious, god bless her. I could here Rab striding up the corridor; his speech was rapid in between coughs. He said he could not go to bed as he had a country to run.

As I lay entombed in my bedroom I missed the family; Miss Rose, Rab, Maggie, Willie and Nellie. I felt isolated, looking at the four walls of my room day after day. The loneliness seeping from me was turning into deep depression. The flu and the sense of being alone in the world had triggered some strange thoughts, paranoid thoughts. However to me they were real, true and I believed them. I felt that the nurses were trying to poison me with their pills. I also thought that someone was trying to kill me. Every time I took my medicine I thought I was going to die. It was very frightening. Can you imagine what it is like lying in bed waiting to be murdered? I pulled the buzzer and the nurse came. I told her my thoughts; she was empathic and promised help for me. Soon after there was a knock on my door, Dr Gérard and a nurse walked into my bedroom. He pulled a chair up to the bed and said he was sorry to hear that I was ill with flu. 'Now Iain' he said 'tell me the problems you've been having with your thoughts.' I told him I felt someone was trying to kill me. Dr Gérard said that I was suffering from auditory hallucinations. The thoughts were not real; he said thoughts could not hurt me. I told him I believed the nurses were trying to poison me with their pills. He said that this was a delusion and part of my illness. I told him it was real to me and I did not believe him. He was very understanding, promising to give me medicine to take the strange thoughts away. If the greatest psychiatrist I have ever known couldn't help me, nobody could. He left.

After about a week the flu symptoms went as quickly as they had come. The nurses said they would escort me to the day room for breakfast. I still felt a little weak and tired. I plodded down to the day room on the stone mosaic floor. I ate a little of the lumpy porridge and then retired to my arm chair with my stewed tea.

Rose and Nellie were present and correct. They had escaped the epidemic. Rab and Willie were present and correct, however Maggie's arm chair was empty. My heart sank. I was frightened to ask where she was however I plucked up the courage and asked. 'Maggie has pneumonia' Rose replied. Don't die on us Maggie, you are our star on the bleakest night, I thought. The world will not be wonderful without you. 'Let's say a prayer for Maggie'. I was uttering an emotional cry to rally the troops. 'I will pray for Maggie' Rose said. Rab joined the ranks saying that he would pray for Maggie. Nellie is too ill to pray, god bless her. I turned to Willie and asked if he would pray for Maggie. 'I don't believe in God, there is no such thing. If there was a God I would not be stuck in the mad house self harming. You can all pray as much as you like, it won't do any good. You are all nuts!' Willie said. 'Alright' I said leave Willie out; each to their own. We prayed day after day for what seemed like an eternity then one morning as I sat in my arm chair the door of the day room swung open, a nurse was pushing a wheel chair and in it, a rather weak and feeble Maggie. We were amazed that all our prayers had been answered. She was whispering what sounded like 'What a wonderful world'. We cheered, tears running down our faces.

Chapter 8 – Burns Night

Todays date is January the twenty fifth 1979, a burns supper is being held in his honour this evening; to celebrate the great Scottish poet. The Scottish songs were playing on the record player and we were all looking forward to the meal of haggis, potatoes and turnip. As we sat around the Formica table we toasted 'The Baird' and his great works. As I looked around at the family they seemed to be enjoying their evening. Rose was sipping a martini, Willie and Rab were having a stiff drink and Maggie had recovered enough to enjoy a sherry. Nellie seemed more disturbed than usual however. My dram went down a treat; the good old whisky tipple. The male orderly stood up and read a poem;

'To a mouse'
Wee sleekit cow'rin tim'rous beastie,
O, what a panic's in thy breastie
Thou need na start awa sae hasty,
Wi bickering brattle!
I wad be laith to rin an' chase thee
Wi murd'ring pattle!

The family cheered the nurse's recital, also praising the greatest Scottish poet who ever lived. A female nurse took over and summarised a few important features of Rabbie Burn's life;

'He was born in Alloway, 2 miles from Ayr on the 25th of January 1759. Burns night is celebrated every year with a Burns supper in Scotland and in places all over the world on his birthday. Rabbie was the eldest of seven children. He lived on a farm and grew up in poverty, his father educated him. At fifteen Rabbie Burns was a labourer. Burns liked the ladies and they inspired his work; to say the least. He also had twelve children. A volume of his work was published in 1786 and it sold for three shillings. He wrote his poems in Scots, Standard English and Scots dialect. Burns went to Edinburgh instead of his original choice of Jamaica as his published book took off. He died at the age of 37 and his body was laid to rest in Dumfries.'

The family thanked the nurse for her few words and clapped profoundly. They raised their glasses in a toast to Rabbie Burns.

As I sat at the red Formica table, thoughts of my restricted life burst into my head. I was a prisoner. I had lost my liberty, being confined. I had been put away, locked away for life. Then came the snakes climbing up my leg, and the voices. The haggis, turnip and potatoes arrived. Looking at the family they were tucking into their meal. Swelling in my gut was uncontrollable agitation. I stood up and knocked the table over. The family stood up, there was food everywhere. Suddenly I was aware of terrible chest pain. Clutching my chest I collapsed onto the day room floor. I heard the nurses shout 'Clear the room!' they sounded the alarm and then phoned the cardiac arrest team. I was vaguely aware of the song 'My love is like a red, red rose' playing in the background. The family were leaving the room. Rose turned and looked at me, our eyes met. What happened to Blackpool I thought? The family were hustled out of the day room. Two nurses were kneeling on the floor next to me, I was slipping away, I heard a voice saying 'Start compressions and mouth to mouth, the doctors are on their way'. I was vaguely aware of someone pressing on my chest and breathing in my mouth, then the deep blackness of death.

In death there will be no suffering. My spirit will be free; my mind will be whole again. God will look after me.

Ian died on the twenty fifth of January 1979. The family of Rose, Willie, Rab, Nellie and Maggie grieved for him. They were his asylum family. The family were informed; the cause of Ian's death was a heart attack. There was a small funeral, attended by Rab, Rose, a couple of the nurses and a male orderly. Ian may you rest in peace.

Dedication A; The Scottish Association of Mental Health (SAMH)

Dedication B; The great support provided by the Community Psychiatric Nurses.

Fiona Park